Focus on

The Bloody Chamber and Other Stories

by Angela Carter

Angela Topping

GREENWICH EXCHANGE
LONDON

Greenwich Exchange, London

Focus on
The Bloody Chamber and Other Stories
© Angela Topping, 2009

First published in Great Britain in 2009
Reprinted 2019
All rights reserved

This book is sold subject to the conditions that it shall not,
by way of trade or otherwise, be lent, resold, hired out
or otherwise circulated without the publisher's prior consent
in any form of binding or cover other than that in which it is published
and without a similar condition including
this condition being imposed on the subsequent purchaser.

Printed and bound by imprintdigital.com
Typesetting and layout by Jude Keen, London
Cover design by December Publications
Tel: 07951511275

Greenwich Exchange Website: www.greenex.co.uk

Cataloguing in Publication Data is available
from the British Library

ISBN: 978-1-906075-25-5

For Tina Threlfall

Special thanks are due to my husband Dave and daughter Rosie for their support, and to Laura Topping, my eldest daughter, for her assistance with feminist criticism. Above all, thanks are due to the late Matt Simpson for giving detailed critical feedback on the drafts, and for his unswerving encouragement of my endeavours.

Contents

1	Miss Lamb, Spotless, Sacrificial	11
2	Surrounded by So Many Mirrors	21
3	Why the Bedclothes So Disordered?	27
4	But it was No Longer a Wolf's Paw	35
5	The Portals of the Great Pines	42
	Further Reading	54

I propose to speak about fairy-stories, though I am aware that this is a rash adventure. Faerie is a perilous land, and in it are pitfalls for the unwary and dungeons for the overbold.

J.R.R. Tolkien

One could argue, I think, that the title The Bloody Chamber itself, alludes in the last analysis not to Bluebeard's meat-locker, nor even to the womb/tomb, but to the human heart.

Lorna Sage

Preface

The Bloody Chamber and Other Stories was first published in 1979. It won the Cheltenham Literary Festival prize and is widely included on Advanced Level and undergraduate programmes of study. Some of the stories had been previously published in journals.

Carter is known as a feminist writer. In *The Bloody Chamber and Other Stories* she writes from a feminist perspective. In many collections of fairy tales, male editors have avoided those stories in which females are triumphant. Carter redresses this in the Virago edition, as does Alison Lurie in her retold selection entitled *Clever Gretchen and Other Stories* (1980). Lurie includes, for example, a version of 'Cap o' Rushes', the English variant of the French 'Cinderella' in which the eponymous heroine solves her own problems, unlike the French version with its fairy godmother. This was known to Shakespeare; it is one of the sources for *King Lear*.

Faerie, according to J.R.R. Tolkien in his essay 'On Fairy-Stories'[1] is 'The Perilous Realm', which 'cannot be caught in a net of words', though his essay is an attempt to define it. It is a world of possibilities and magic:

> The realm of fairy-story is wide and deep and high and filled with many things: all manner of beasts and birds are found there; shoreless seas and stars uncounted; beauty that is an enchantment, and an ever-present peril; both joy and sorrow as sharp as swords.

Carter's settings mostly draw on the conventions of Faerie; many of them use the liminal space of 'woods', as the *Märchen* (the German term for fairy stories) do. Some of them are more frighteningly set in the real world. 'The Bloody Chamber' is one such: the Marquis' castle has a telephone and a *fin-de-siècle* setting. 'Puss-in-Boots', other than having a talking cat as the narrator, is another.

The stories, although quite different from each other, work as a collection because they are all inspired by traditional fairy stories. Carter had translated Perrault and was inspired by his versions. Fairy tales, like many other good things, were not primarily intended for children; many of the originals are violent and distressing, as can be seen if one reads *The Virago Books of Fairy Tales* which Carter edited. Fairy and folk tales originated as part of the oral tradition and were collected in the nineteenth century but toned down by overly well-meaning editors and eventually appropriated by children. *The Bloody Chamber and Other Stories* gives *Märchen* back into adult readership: the collection is both sexualised and violent. Many writers have drawn on the traditional stories, such as Oscar Wilde, Gabriel Garcia Marquez, Margaret Atwood. Carter is in good company. Terri Windling and Ellen Datlow, in their introduction to *Black Thorn, White Rose*, a book of modern adult fairy tales, compare the literary fairy story to jazz:

> The literary fairy story, like jazz, is an improvisation on a theme. ... Like jazz, it is best appreciated by those with an ear for the melody on which it is based. The pleasure lies in savoring the writer's skill as he or she transforms a familiar story.[2]

It is important to realise that Carter did not see herself as writing 'versions'.[3] Instead she used traditional stories as a starting point for new texts, drawing on some of the characters and plot lines, adding other elements, such as Gothic horror, to the mix. It is recommended that readers familiarise themselves with these traditional stories and firmly separate them from the versions shown in the films made by the Disney Corporation. *The Bloody Chamber and Other Stories* is far removed from such sanitised and simplistic representations. 'The Bloody Chamber', the title story, draws on 'Bluebeard' just as Dickens' 'Captain Murderer' relates to it. 'Beauty and the Beast' inspires both 'The Courtship of Mr Lyon' and 'The Tiger's Bride'. The source for 'Puss-in-Boots' is obvious; though Carter's story is very different, the idea of an intelligent boot-wearing cat links the tale to its fairy-story counterpart. 'The Erl-King' uses a character from folk tale and ballad, a goblin or sprite of the woodlands. 'The Snow Child' has clear links to 'Snow White and Rose Red' and 'The Lady of the House of Love' references 'The Sleeping Beauty' but has a beautiful vampire as its central character, in a clever reinterpretation of the story. 'The Werewolf', 'The Company of Wolves' and 'Wolf-Alice' all take their inspiration from 'Little Red Riding Hood' combined with the Werewolf myth. The latter takes the name of the child protagonist from *Alice in Wonderland* and *Through the Looking-Glass, and What Alice Found There*, which themselves draw on elements of fantasy. Carter also owes something to the Gothic novel genre such as *The Castle of Otranto* by Horace Walpole (1764), which is considered to be the first of its kind, determining elements such as the supernatural, murder, secrets, settings of castles and ruined abbeys and so on. 'The Bloody Chamber' title story itself belongs to this genre. The Gothic novels of the nineteenth century, such as *Frankenstein* by Mary Shelley and *Dracula* by Bram Stoker, are very much part of the literary milieu in which Carter is writing.

The literary fairy story is a respected genre which came to prominence in the nineteenth century. Thackeray, Ruskin, George MacDonald, Dickens, Oscar Wilde, Hans Christian Andersen and many others delighted in writing new fairy tales at the same time that collectors and editors like the Grimm brothers were rescuing for posterity the versions they were told. Andrew Lang compiled his beautiful series of fairy-tale collections, with titles such as *The Blue Fairy Book* (1889), *The Red Fairy Book* (1890). The Romantic poets were inspired by them, for example Keats' stunning 'La Belle Dame sans Merci' and Tennyson's much-loved 'The Lady of Shallot', both still firm favourites with children and adults alike. Coleridge's 'Kubla Khan' and 'The Ancient Mariner' are also pervaded by an enchanted and magical tone. Carter is continuing a noble tradition at the same time as producing unique texts, some of which offer a feminist reinterpretation of motifs from the old tales. The literary fairy story is the precursor of the fantasy genre, exemplified by the more recent writing of J.R.R Tolkien, Philip Pullman and J.K. Rowling, to name only a few amongst the many.

The stories are not dealt with singly in this book, as throughout the collection there is subtle interplay between them. Carter is constructing a dialogue, trying different approaches to the same questions. Anny Crunelle-Vanrigh, in her essay 'The Logic of the Same and *Différance*',[4] put it this way:

> The fixed meaning guaranteed by the extra-systemic metaphysics of (male) presence is replaced by a game of *différance*, of volatile and unstable identity – beast or beauty, tiger or bride, wolf or girl – in which the new identity/signifier can in a sense be said to give meaning to the previous one and so on …

Accordingly, this commentary selects different strands of Carter's explorations: the notion of women as prey; identity through masks and mirrors; sex; transformations; settings. As we shall see, Carter often draws on the work of other writers: she was a great reader. The stories are startling, inventive and dialectical. It should be read in conjunction with the stories and opens up a dialogue with the reader, who is encouraged to form his or her own hypotheses in response to these dark and imaginative stories written in Carter's inimitable, jewelled, baroque prose.

Notes

1. J.R.R. Tolkien *Tree and Leaf,* Unwin, 1964.

2. Ellen Datlow and Terri Windling (eds.), *Black Thorn, White Rose,* Avon Books (USA), 1994.

3. "My intention was not to do 'versions' or, as the American edition of the book said, horribly, 'adult' fairy tales, but to extract the latent content from the traditional stories and to use it as the beginnings of new stories." Interview with Carter quoted in *Guardian* review of 24 June 2006, 'Femme Fatale'.

4. *Journal of Fairy Tale Studies.* 12, 1 (1998), Issue on 'Angela Carter and the Literary *Märchen*' (guest editors: Cristina Bacchilega and Danielle M. Roemer). Reprinted in *Angela Carter and the Fairy Tale,* Wayne State University Press, 1998.

1

Miss Lamb, Spotless, Sacrificial

One of the main themes in *The Bloody Chamber and Other Stories* is the initiation of a female protagonist into womanhood by placing her into a situation which requires power and resourcefulness. In the traditional stories Carter uses as a source, the female characters are often presented as victims, or as being helpless against male figures such as 'the big bad wolf'. There are traditional stories which show women in a more positive light, but these tend to be less well known. Carter turns these stereotypes on their heads. As a feminist, Carter often presents women as strong and independent. Many of her female characters have to develop assertiveness and ruthlessness in order to survive. Margaret Atwood goes so far as to say, in her essay 'Running with Tigers',[1] that

> It is Carter's contention that a certain amount of tigerishness may be necessary if women are to achieve an independent … existence; if they are to avoid – at the extreme end of passivity – becoming meat.

Becoming meat or prey is literally what some of these protagonists face. There is a link to fairy stories here, as often they are cautionary tales too. Little Red Riding Hood, for example, is in strong danger of becoming meat, and in some versions she actually does. However, in Carter's own stories based on this tale, 'The Werewolf' and 'The Company of Wolves', the red-capped heroine can and does take care of herself, in the former, cutting off the paw of the wolf, and in the latter, becoming its mate.

'The Bloody Chamber' is the longest story in the collection, and also the title story. It is voiced by the female protagonist, a girl of seventeen, who is marrying an older man. She imagines she loves him, but is equally attracted by his money. Her family (herself, her widowed mother and her old nurse) is living in desperate poverty. Partly to escape this, she unwittingly casts herself in the role of sacrificial virgin in the hands of a sadistic man. The warning signs are there from the start. The wedding dress is "wrapped up in tissue paper and red ribbon like a Christmas gift of crystallised fruit". 'Tissue' connotes flesh, the meaning of red is obvious, and the simile of "crystallised fruit" hints that she herself is seen by him as a delicious sweetmeat. It also suggests the notion of preserving, which foreshadows what the girl finds in the bloody chamber: the bodies of the former, murdered wives in a bizarre display arranged for the man's private enjoyment. Carter's use of the red and white symbolism here is similar to that of Hardy's *Tess of the d'Urbervilles,* in which his female protagonist is destroyed by two men who profess love for her. Hardy is sympathetic to the female plight but portrays women as weak and passive, the victims of the 'President of the Immortals', Hardy's personification of fate. Carter arms females with intelligence, resourcefulness and sometimes actual weapons. In 'The Company of Wolves', the Little Red Riding Hood figure 'has her knife and is afraid of nothing'. She ends the story in the wolf's embrace, not his stomach. The mother of the speaker in 'The Bloody Chamber' keeps an "antique service revolver ... in her reticule". It is this weapon she uses to kill the murderous husband in the nick of time. This deed is prefigured by the mention of her shooting a man-eating tiger before the age of seventeen, as only one of a range of extra-ordinary achievements. She is a mother who is utterly ruthless when it comes to protecting her child. In Perrault's[2] version, it is the bride's brothers who rescue her; Carter shifts the emphasis to women taking care of themselves and each other.

The use of red and white juxtapositions becomes clearer and more marked as the story continues. The engagement ring is a fire opal, which has flashes of red in its milky innocence. Later, when the Marquis is about to execute her, these fires 'had died down', linking them with her imagined love for him, which is now dead. His wedding gift is a choker (again a prefiguration of death, and one of the brides has indeed been strangled) of rubies, compared to 'an extraordinarily precious slit throat'. The history given is interesting:

> After the Terror, in the early days of the Directory, the aristos who'd escaped the guillotine had an ironic fad of tying a red ribbon round their necks at just the point where the blade would have sliced it through, a red ribbon like the memory of a wound. And his grandmother, taken with the notion, had her ribbon made up in rubies; such a gesture of luxurious defiance!

This makes the symbolism cleverly ambiguous. The ruby choker seems a dangerous ill omen, especially when it becomes uncomfortable, or she is ordered to wear it when she is deflowered, but it could also represent survival, as it was worn by those who had escaped the guillotine. It also connotes slavery and female subjugation. The girl wears the necklace to the opera, accessorising a white dress, and the combination is clearly sacrificial: "… the white dress, the frail child within it; and the flashing crimson jewels round her neck, bright as arterial blood." To underline this implication, the fiancé watches her in the mirror "with the assessing eye … of a housewife in the market, inspecting cuts on the slab". This is an explicit reference to the idea of the female as meat. Its literalness is a shocking critique of the way society views women, as in advertisements, beauty contests or semi-naked models in popular newspapers, which aim to please the male gaze and are seen by feminists as degrading to women.

Red and white also appear separately. The husband always reminds the girl of lilies, which are associated with death. Carter describes lilies in a necrophiliac manner which makes the husband sound both attractive and strangely repellent at the same time:

> Possessed of that strange ominous calm of a sentient vegetable, like one of those cobra-headed, funereal lilies whose white sheaths are curled out of a flesh, as thick and tensely yielding to the touch as vellum.

The impression created is one of heavy white flesh which is unpleasant to touch. It has sexual undertones (she could be describing a penis) as well as animalistic ones, vellum being animal skin. This makes him sound inhuman, or like a hunting animal. Further suggestions of his role as hunter follow, such as the "smell of Russian leather" which gives him away when he tries to creep up on her, the "dark mane" of hair, "heavy eyelids", his soft tread "as if all his shoes had soles of velvet" and "leonine shape of his head". The way he fills her bedchamber with lilies makes it feel as though she is invading his lair. Their whiteness is not a whiteness of innocence, but a pallor of death, "undertakers' lilies with the heavy pollen". These are the sort of lilies that "stain you", just as the girl is stained by the Marquis. The bloodstained sheets are a traditional sign of lost virginity but also prefigure the sacrificial rite which he intends for her. There are many other instances of these two colours being used both in conjunction and separately, even down to tiny details like the red chairs in the opera house, or the crowd parting "like the Red Sea". The most significant of them is the red mark from the stained key to the bloody chamber, which cannot be washed off the key or from the girl's forehead when the Marquis presses it on her face. She bears this mark, which is similar to a bindi, for the rest of her life. A red bindi is worn by married Hindu women over the site of the supposed third eye. This is the site of concealed wisdom, which the girl possesses now that she has seen inside the bloody chamber and her innocence has been replaced with a knowing experience which allows her to protect herself. She has moved from victimhood to a position of power. To use Atwood's word, she has become more "tigerish". If we take Blake's exploration of Innocence and Experience through the binary oppositions (or "contraries" as Blake calls them in *The Marriage of Heaven and Hell*)[3] of 'The Lamb' and 'The Tyger' in *Songs of Innocence and Experience*, we can see what Carter is doing. She is not valuing one over the other; she is suggesting that they are two states of womanhood. Innocence is vulnerable but has its own strengths; however, experience is needed to survive the world. The two states of womanhood must work together: it is the mother's intuition which senses that her child is in trouble. The inner strength of innocence is a force to be reckoned with too. The mother came because "I never heard you cry before … not when you were happy." The girl, retelling her story to the reader, seems remarkably calm and level-headed. By the end of the story, she has inherited fabulous wealth from the Marquis and spent it wisely, and is well on her way to emulating her mother's courage and resourcefulness. Kathleen E.B. Manley sees the female protagonist in this story as a "woman in process". In her essay 'The Woman in Process in Angela Carter's "The Bloody Chamber"', she argues:

> Some readers of Angela Carter's 'The Bloody Chamber' have seen its narrator-protagonist as a passive young woman who makes little attempt to avoid her apparent fate. Several features of the text, however, suggest that the protagonist is rather a woman in process, a person who oscillates between passivity and action.[4]

The girl recognises she has fallen into the trap laid by the Marquis, but she does not accept her fate. Her innocence has proved dangerous; it has made her desirable as prey. At the end of the story she is living with her mother and the blind piano tuner. She is no longer an object of male gaze: the piano tuner loves her for herself, not as an object in a museum arranged to please the eye of a male who enjoys sadistic pornography. The choice of a blind man for her ally and new lover is a deliberate way of reinforcing this point.

Another story in which the female protagonist moves from innocence to experience is 'The Courtship of Mr Lyon'. However, Mr Lyon is a very different character from the Marquis. The Marquis is fully human but behaves like a beast of prey; Mr Lyon is a gentleman who behaves sensitively and kindly but has the outward appearance of a lion. This story is very different in tone from 'The Bloody Chamber', which owes a good deal to the horror genre.[5] 'The Courtship of Mr Lyon' is a tender and touching story, just as its inspiration, 'Beauty and the Beast' is. Beauty's father is one in a line of ineffective fathers in this collection, and he relinquishes his daughter easily to the Beast, just as his slapdash business practices have made him lose his money. Beauty's innocence is represented by the white rose her father steals from the garden of the Beast. The rose is described as:

> one last, single, perfect rose that might have been the last rose left living in all the white winter, and of so delicate and intense a fragrance that it seemed to ring like a dulcimer on the frozen earth.

Carter's deployment of synaesthesia[6] here makes the rose seem remarkable and unique, like Beauty. The photograph of her that her father shows to Mr Lyon makes Beauty seem special, as he regards it "with a strange kind of wonder". Male gaze this may be, but Beauty's face is full of clear-sightedness, and it seems that she is admired for this quality rather than her facial features: "The camera had captured a certain look she had, sometimes, of absolute sweetness and absolute gravity, as if her eyes might pierce appearances and see your soul." Beauty possesses the prized quality of innocence, and perhaps this appeals to Mr Lyon. He may hope that she may be able to see beyond his physical appearance to the gentle nature within. However, he is not without beauty himself, but it is a feral, strange beauty: "… a lion is a lion and a man is a man and, though lions are more beautiful by far than we are, yet they belong to a different order of beauty …" At first she is afraid of him, and expresses the idea that she is meat for his meal: "when she saw the great paws lying on the arm of his chair, she thought: they are the death of any tender herbivore. And such a one she felt herself to be, Miss Lamb, spotless, sacrificial." She is mistaken, however: it is she who has the power to hurt or heal him, through her innocence. He treats her kindly and engages her in conversation, behaving like a perfect gentleman until she is "chattering away to him as if she had known him all her life". As with 'The Bloody Chamber', clues are given which indicate the nature of the beast. Beauty lives in the utmost luxury. Mr Lyon's house is elegant: "Palladian", elegantly furnished, and she is served with the best-quality food. Mr Lyon's voice is compared to an organ, "an instrument created to inspire the terror that the great chords of organs bring", which seems closer to awe than fear. The subtle religious undertones are firmly anchored by the reference to St Mark's gospel following almost immediately in the text: "she thought of the first great beast of the Apocalypse, the winged lion with his paw on the Gospel, St Mark." This is further delineated by his appearance when the fire they are sitting in front of "irradiates" him, giving the appearance of a "halo". One is unmistakably reminded of Aslan in C.S. Lewis' *Chronicles of Narnia*,[7] which of course is another notable literary fairy story. In this allegorical work, Aslan represents Christ. Carter also draws on Blake to demonstrate the nobility of the lion. Blake has a lion acting as a kindly protector in *Songs of Innocence and Experience,* in 'The Little Girl Lost', who has a "mane of gold" and who licks Lyca just as Mr Lyon licks Beauty.[8] In a sense, many of Carter's protagonists are "little girls lost", adrift in the troubled waters of Experience and abandoned by inept or missing fathers. This licking is Mr Lyon's way of expressing his love, but he subjugates himself to Beauty's innocence and trust:

> ... he flung himself at her feet and buried his head in her lap ... she felt his hot breath on her fingers, the stiff bristles of his muzzle grazing her skin, the rough lapping of his tongue and then, with a flood of compassion, understood: all he is doing is kissing my hands.

It is as though she has tamed him, but when he leaves the room, he goes on "all fours". Beauty leaves him to go and visit her father in London. She loses her innocence and beauty here as the world of luxury spoils and corrupts her. She becomes selfish and loses her sweetness: "Her face was acquiring, instead of beauty, a lacquer of that invisible prettiness that characterises certain pampered, expensive cats." To save both herself and Mr Lyon, she has to return to a state of innocence, an innocence born out of experience, a rejection of the monetary values of the city and an acceptance of love, and the otherness of Mr Lyon. She has to learn compassion. She has to return to him out of choice and kiss his paws as he once kissed her hands. He rejects his lion shape, and his "meat-hook claws" become fingers. "He was no longer a lion in her arms but a man." Carter recalls the ballad 'Tam Lin'[9] here, when Janet of Carterhaugh must hold on to Tam Lin while the fairies who wish to keep him in enslavement try to change him into frightening shapes. Her love conquers all, and she eventually holds a naked man in her arms. Beauty's innocence and love protect her from becoming meat, and the apparent beast is a noble man. On one level, Carter is teaching us that some men are evil and others are good, but one cannot tell by appearances. The wolf in 'Little Red Riding Hood' is smooth and charming when she first meets him, just like the Marquis in 'The Bloody Chamber'.

But women can be beasts too. In 'The Tiger's Bride', the narrator's useless (as a protector) father loses her to the beast at cards. She avoids becoming meat by joining him and becoming an animal. This is because she sees more value and honesty in the animal world than the human world. All the beast desires is to see her naked. At first, she refuses and is held captive until she agrees. The time of captivity allows Carter some space for her heroine to reflect on the ways of the human world. In the house of the beast there are no human servants; she is waited on by a clockwork doll that has been made in her image. This is a clever symbol for the way the girl is perceived in male-dominated society: "That clockwork girl who powdered my cheeks for me: had I not been allotted the same kind of imitative life amongst men that the doll-maker had given her?" It is only by being removed from this limiting world that she can discover herself, and lose the limitations placed on her. She no longer sees herself as a mannequin. Once she has realised this, the clockwork doll ceases to resemble her. She contemplates sending the clockwork doll back to her father in her place, though she doubts he would notice, since he has never looked at her properly. Another view of society she rejects is the notion that, like animals, women have no souls:

> … all the best religions in the world state categorically that not beasts nor women were equipped with the flimsy insubstantial things when the good Lord opened the gates of Eden and let Eve and her familiars tumble out.

To align herself with the beast, then, is to find her true companionship, by means of a process of logic based on the flawed suppositions of the patriarchal world which has let her down and disrespected her. Her intelligence has been denied because she is "a young woman, a virgin, and therefore men denied me rationality". The beast seems to respect her, even though he originally wanted her as an object of male gaze: he learns from her, and shows himself to her first. Like Mr Lyon, he is described as beautiful, though savage and powerful; it is a beauty distinct from human beauty, altogether 'other':

> A great feline, tawny shape whose pelt was barred with a savage geometry of bars the colour of burned wood. His domed, heavy head, so terrible he must hide it. How subtle the muscles, how profound the tread. The annihilating vehemence of his eyes, like twin suns.

Instead of full sentences here, Carter uses a list, to illustrate the girl's gaze, as she takes in the different aspects of the animal. The imagery is drawn from fire and heat. How like Blake's tiger, which "burns bright" and whose eyes "burnt" in "distant skies"! Carter's tiger cries two diamond tears for the girl, which turn back into water when she becomes a tiger. In Blake's poem "the stars threw down their spears/And watered heaven with their tears." Carter is making explicit, pointed references to *Songs of Innocence and Experience*. The god of the tiger is the same as the god who made the Lamb. This undercuts brilliantly the shabby ideas of the 'best religions' which in their arrogance deny that women and beasts have souls. The girl finds her commonality with the tiger, in a neat reversal of another biblical reference: "The tiger will never lie down with the lamb; he acknowledges no pact that is not reciprocal. The lamb must learn to run with the tigers." The girl's conquering of her fear and recognising that the tiger feared her more than she feared him, allows her to be reborn as a more powerful being, one who knows herself and can acknowledge her desires. She avoids becoming meat just as the girl does in 'The Company of Wolves' , by lying down with the beast and understanding the beast within herself. The tiger licks the girl into her new self in a rebirth experience. Instead of seeing herself as 'the cold white meat of contract', she becomes a creature in control of her own life. The girl in 'The Company of Wolves' knows no fear either but joins forces with the beast in a strange marriage. Beauty feels compassion and guilt for Mr Lyon, and the girl in 'The Bloody Chamber' works through her fear and lives on after the Marquis has been brought to his deserved end by a vengeful mother. These women have liberated themselves and rejected passivity. They are survivors.

Notes

1   Margaret Atwood, 'Running with Tigers', in *Essays on the Art of Angela Carter: Flesh and the Mirror*, edited by Lorna Sage, Virago, 1994.

2   Charles Perrault is a French writer (1628–1703). He was the founder of the literary fairy tale and wrote many of the most popular tales, such as 'La Belle au bois dormant' (Sleeping Beauty). Carter translated these stories into English (1977 and 1982).

3   "Without contraries is no progression." *The Marriage of Heaven and Hell* (1793).

4   *Journal of Fairy Tale Studies*, 12, 1 (1998), issue on 'Angela Carter and the Literary *Märchen*' (guest editors: Cristina Bacchilega and Danielle M. Roemer). Reprinted in *Angela Carter and the Fairy Tale*, Wayne State University Press, 1998.

5   Horror genre is fiction written with the intention to scare and disquiet the reader, for example *Dracula* by Bram Stoker, (1897), *Frankenstein* by Mary Shelley (1818) and other works.

6   The use of one sense to describe another.

7   "He's wild, you know. Not like a tame lion." *The Lion, The Witch and The Wardrobe* by C.S. Lewis (1950).

8 In futurity
I prophesy
That the earth from sleep
(Grave the sentence deep)

Shall arise, and seek
For her Maker meek;
And the desert wild
Become a garden mild.

In the southern clime,
Where the summer's prime
Never fades away,
Lovely Lyca lay.

Seven summers old
Lovely Lyca told.
She had wandered long,
Hearing wild birds' song.

'Sweet sleep, come to me,
Underneath this tree;
Do father, mother, weep?
Where can Lyca sleep?

'Lost in desert wild
Is your little child.
How can Lyca sleep
If her mother weep?

'If her heart does ache,
Then let Lyca wake;
If my mother sleep,
Lyca shall not weep.

'Frowning, frowning night,
O'er this desert bright
Let thy moon arise,
While I close my eyes.'

Sleeping Lyca lay,
While the beasts of prey,
Come from caverns deep,
Viewed the maid asleep.

The kingly lion stood,
And the virgin viewed:
Then he gambolled round
O'er the hallowed ground.

Leopards, tigers, play
Round her as she lay;
While the lion old
Bowed his mane of gold,

And her bosom lick,
And upon her neck,
From his eyes of flame,
Ruby tears there came;

While the lioness
Loosed her slender dress,
And naked they conveyed
To caves the sleeping maid.

9 *The English and Scottish Popular Ballads,* ed. Francis James Child.

2

Surrounded by So Many Mirrors

Carter uses mirrors, reflections and masks as motifs to raise and address questions about identity, how we see ourselves and how others see us. An earlier story, 'Flesh and the Mirror', indicates her interest in the notion of reflections as a way of revealing identity and self-awareness. The same motif is developed two years later in *The Magic Toyshop* (Virago, 1981), when Melanie, the protagonist, becomes obsessed with posing naked in the mirror as part of her adolescent exploration of who she is and who she might become. *The Bloody Chamber* collection offers different variations on the theme. In 'Wolf-Alice', the eponymous feral child finds a mirror in the house of the Duke, a vampiric werewolf. She reacts to it as an animal would. She sniffs it, tries to fight it, and is bemused when it copies her gestures. It becomes a companion, a "littermate": "In spite of this barrier, she was lonely enough to ask this creature to try to play with her, baring her teeth and grinning; at once she received a reciprocal invitation." This encounter happens at the time of her first menstruation and is also linked explicitly to the moon. She even wonders whether she is seeing the beast who bites her in the night to make her bleed. Because the moon regulates the menstrual cycle, this surmise is symbolically correct, so the irony is multi-layered. At first, she cannot see beyond the mirror to her true self but as her dawning self-awareness grows, she looks behind the mirror, round the back, and realises: "… her companion was, in fact, no more than a particularly ingenious version of the shadow she cast on sunlit grass." She accepts this, and her relationship with the mirror changes now she knows it is herself. It leads to her beginning to wear clothes, and washing off her ashes, calling to mind both 'Ashputtel' and its other versions, 'Cap o' Rushes' and 'Cinderella', the latter a Perrault tale. It helps her to find who she is as a woman as well as a human. Tellingly, the werewolf Duke is not reflected in his bedroom mirror, just the "disordered covers" of his bed. However, when he is shot by the silver bullet, Wolf-Alice tends the Duke by licking his wound. Carter describes the mirror as "rational" and so it cannot reflect a werewolf or a vampire. However, as Wolf-Alice licks the wound, she heals him, which results in his gaining a reflection:

> Little by little there appeared in [the mirror], like the image on photographic paper that emerges first, a formless web of tracery, the prey caught in its own net, then in firmer yet still shadowed outline until at last, as vivid as real life itself, as if brought into being by her soft, moist, gentle, tongue, finally, the face of the Duke.

The child reared by wolves, having found her humanity and womanhood, is able to heal the werewolf of his condition, through the redemption of her nurturing love. The licking is a rebirth into humanity. The ending of 'The Tiger's Bride' is a mirror image of 'Wolf-Alice' when the tiger licks off her skin: "And each stroke of his tongue ripped off skin after successive skin, all the skins of a life in the world, and left behind a nascent patina of shining hairs." The protagonist prefers to become an animal, because the human world has let her down by restricting and oppressing her. When she first meets the tiger, he is wearing a mask to conceal his true identity and appear human. The removal of the mask allows the protagonist to see him as he really is: vulnerable yet "heraldic", whereas in his mask he is "two-dimensional" and "beautiful … but with too much formal symmetry of feature to be entirely human". Carter reveals what is hidden behind masks; true selves are more interesting than a façade of civilised lies.

Carter offers a plurality of outcomes which mirror each other in different images. In 'The Lady of the House of Love', the protagonist is a vampire, and as such, lacks a reflection. She is afraid of mirrors: her servant has to keep them away from her, and the 'cracked mirror' on the wall offers no reflection, no self-knowledge for the lady trapped in the castle, who is forced to feast on her occasional visitors. The character is strongly reminiscent of Miss Havisham in Dickens' *Great Expectations* as she wears "an antique bridal gown" and "sits alone in her high dark house" and "industrious spiders have woven canopies in the corners of this ornate and rotting palace." Like Havisham, she preys on young men, rather more literally. She is undone by kindness, as the bicyclist she intends to consume tastes her blood, in attempting to treat an accidental wound. The Erl-King, too, is conquered by love, in a way. The Little Red Riding Hood figure falls in love with him, but has to strangle him to protect herself, as she knows he plans to cage her for food. She is able to do this because he trusts her enough to lie in her lap. For her, it is his eyes which are mesmeric, because she can see herself in them. Carter uses the reflection in the eyes of the Erl-King to symbolise the danger the female is in:

> Your green eye is a reducing chamber. If I look into it long enough, I will become as small as my own reflection. I will diminish to a point and vanish. I will be drawn down into that black whirlpool and be consumed by you.

She recognises his charm, but resists it. The Erl-King represents men who use charm and guile to control women. She refuses to succumb. Carter compares the eyes to green amber, which traps bugs and fossilises them. Here reflections are double-edged; they serve to warn but are also part of the trap. The 'reducing chamber' is a hint of what has happened in the past with other young girls. When she frees his birds, they turn back into the young women he has trapped. The protagonist was clearly intended for the same fate. The eyes have a hypnotic force. The other girls were drawn into them, and reduced to caged singing birds, waiting to be eaten. The mirror of his eyes is a reductive one. The Erl-King is reminiscent of the Marquis in the title story, who also hopes to reduce the female protagonist to an object for his consumption.

In a sense, the clockwork maid in 'The Tiger's Bride' acts as a mirror, as she is the mirror image of the girl. Once the girl has rejected her dependency on her father, and found her inner beast, the doll ceases to look like her. The machine, which carries a looking glass, has allowed the girl to re-evaluate herself. It takes her a minute to realise she is looking at herself, just as Wolf-Alice had to realise the same thing when she encounters the mirror: "… it takes me a while to recognise her, in her little cap, her white stockings, her frilled petticoats." The looking-glass carried by the maid-machine has magical properties. It reveals to her what her father is doing, which allows her to see that she owes him nothing; that he does not care for her and does not miss her; he is now winning at cards, which is all he cared about. She loses her sense of dependence and duty, which frees her from any filial obligation, so she can pursue her own life. She takes the mirror from the maid, seeing not her own face, but her father's, smiling:

> … at first I thought he was smiling at me. Then I saw he was smiling with pure gratification. He sat, I saw, in the parlour of our lodgings, at the very table where he had lost me, but now he was busy counting out a tremendous pile of banknotes.

She can see that his bags are packed. He is willing and ready to leave her behind. When she looks in the mirror again, she does not know herself. She has ceased to be a daughter; the mirror has revealed 'a pale, hollow-eyed girl'. Her new separateness from her father allows her to become more fully herself, a free agent. She chooses the beast, who at least wants her, and has been true to her. What she sees in the mirror appears to be revelatory, but the mirror is magical and capable of tricking her. It could show a possible event, as a crystal ball is meant to do or it could merely be reflecting her innermost desires. But she naively puts her faith in the truth of the mirror and rejects her father, as he has rejected her.

In 'The Courtship of Mr Lyon', the mirror is a truth-teller. Before she leaves Mr Lyon to go to London to visit her father, Beauty sees herself reflected in the beast's eyes, just as the girl was in 'The Erl-King', though with a less sinister effect: "He drew back his head and gazed at her with his green inscrutable eyes, in which she saw her face repeated twice, as small as if it were in bud." The natural imagery here, of the "bud", recalls the white rose that her father stole. "Small" here stands for delicate and hopeful, as opposed to the smallness in the Erl-King's eyes, which implies shrinking and annihilation. Beauty still deserves her name in the eyes of the beast. However, in London she loses her modesty. Pampered by her now prosperous father, she becomes vain. The mirror becomes her flatterer:

> You could not have said that her freshness was fading but she smiled at herself in mirrors a little too often, these days, and the face that smiled back was not quite the one that she had seen contained in the beast's agate eyes.

Carter makes it explicit that she is not the person she was, that she is less lovely because her inner loveliness has been tarnished. To regain this inner beauty, she needs to return to the beast, to offer love, to put others before herself. The visit from the beast's spaniel breaks 'the trance' of the mirror, its seductive powers fail in the face of a crisis: the beast is dying. She returns to save him and from this point mirrors cease to figure in the story. Vanity is a distraction; outward appearance is shallow and immaterial.

The oppressive and sinister atmosphere in 'The Bloody Chamber', and the seventeen-year-old protagonist's search for identity, are merged in a stunning use of mirrors. She sees herself in a new way in the mirror at the opera house, and in the bride's boudoir mirrors are everywhere. The bed is the central point, as if the Marquis has set a perverted voyeuristic stage to enable him to see her being deflowered from a variety of angles: "Our bed. And surrounded by so many mirrors! Mirrors on all the walls, in stately frames of contorted gold, that reflected more white lilies than I'd ever seen in my life before." Carter's use of minor sentences here creates a sense of listing, as the bride takes in her new surroundings. The word "contorted" suggests discomfort and links it to sadistic sex, and the white lilies are at once funereal and sexual, with their heavy scent and their potency, as the Marquis reminds her of lilies. He points out that the mirrors make his one bride look like a "harem", reinforcing the sexual implications and foreshadowing the plans he has for her to join his harem of dead flesh hidden in the bloody chamber.

Kathleen E.B. Manley[1] sees the mirrors in this story as a means of assisting the protagonist to reach self-knowledge: "The mirrors, by providing opportunities to see herself as others see her, allow the protagonist to begin to have a more complete sense of herself as subject." As an example, Manley cites the mirrors at the opera, in which the protagonist thinks she sees herself through the eyes of the Marquis. His male gaze is made sinister by the metaphor of a "connoisseur inspecting horseflesh" and his monocle, which makes one eye appear monstrous. At first, she notices him watching her, so that the mirrors become an agent of her spying on him. But then she looks at herself. Although she looks like a sacrificial victim (ironically, this is how he does see her) she suddenly realises that she too has a "capacity for corruption". There is a dual meaning here, which allows Carter to create an irony. The protagonist means sexual corruption. Female desire can lead to depravity just as male desire can: pornography is not just a male preserve, nor is libido. However, the meaning which is more likely from the Marquis' viewpoint, is the corruptibility of the flesh by torture and death, the fate he has in mind for her, in his necrophiliac prison. As Manley says: "the Marquis favors a dichotomy between innocence and debauchery, not innocence and experience."[2] The fact that the protagonist gains experience and survives is a victory over his sadism and depravity.

In the mirrors in her bedroom, the girl sees herself "become that multitude of girls ... identical in their chic navy blue tailor-mades". This somehow diminishes her, makes her feel nothing special. The "dozen husbands" reflected in the mirrors make him, conversely, seem even more dominant, because he is taking the initiative and "unwrapping" her, a "ritual from the brothel", which implies voyeurism, although he is watching himself with her. Looking in the mirror when he has stripped her naked, she is immediately reminded of some sadistic, paedophilic pornography he had shown her "when our engagement permitted us to be alone together". The mirror shows her the truth: namely that her husband is a "lecher", and if that is not clear enough to the reader, just like the Marquis, the man in the etching wears a monocle. She, however, remains unaware of the link, though she is "aghast" at her arousal. When he does eventually bed her, the mirrors reflect "a dozen husbands" as they "'impaled a dozen brides". The violence of the act, intensified by the word "impaled" is magnified in the mirrors, which have now become a sex aid for his jaded appetite. Afterwards, though, she wonders if she is seeing him at last as he really is, "without his mask"; she truly sees him as he really is only when she has seen the contents of the bloody chamber itself. The veneer of civilisation glosses over his evil intent only as long as he wishes it to do so. One of his former wives has been literally impaled by the iron maiden in the bloody chamber. Mirrors warn and point out truths to the protagonist, which have to be decoded as she explores the depth of her husband's murderous depravity.

The motifs of mirrors, reflections and masks are deployed cleverly by Carter to explore the theme of identity in these stories, in the same way as they are used in fairy stories. The question "Mirror, mirror on the wall, who is fairest of them all?" from traditional variants of 'The Sleeping Beauty' is developed to include "who is the most wicked of all" and "who am I?"

Notes

1   *Journal of Fairy Tale Studies*, 12, 1 (1998), issue on 'Angela Carter and the Literary *Märchen*' (guest editors: Cristina Bacchilega and Danielle M. Roemer). Reprinted in *Angela Carter and the Fairy Tale*, Wayne State University Press, 1998.

2   Ibid.

3

Why the Bedclothes So Disordered?

At the time of writing *The Bloody Chamber and Other Stories,* Carter had been reading the writings of the Marquis de Sade, from whose name the term 'sadism' is derived. He believed in the pursuit of his own pleasure as the highest principle, regardless of morality. The Marquis in the title story is an example of what he advocated. Andrea Dworkin, in *Pornography: Men Possessing Women* (1979) sees de Sade as a typical misogynistic pornographer. Margaret Atwood, in her essay 'Running with Tigers', values Carter as presenting an opposition to de Sade:

> Carter attacks the subject of de Sade in much the same way that de Sade himself may have attacked the chambermaids: with suavity, wit, no-holds-barred intelligence, panache, bravado, stiletto-like epigrams, and sudden disconcerting pounces. One of the things that really interests her is the reductionist nature of pornography as a form ... [1]

It is inevitable that Carter, as a feminist writer, would explore sex as a theme in her work. The role of a woman in the sex act has often been presented as passive, or as one of awe-struck wonder at the marvellous work that is a man, according, for example, to anonymous Victorian pornography such as *The Adventures of a Schoolboy* (1866) and *My Secret Life* (1888), in which the male protagonists visit coy prostitutes or seduce and deflower young girls. By contrast, Carter presents female libido as active: women can be as lustful and predatory as men, just as governed by animal impulses, just as bestial. 'Puss-in-Boots' represents women as able to enjoy sex, and take the lead; 'The Snow Child' is ambiguous; 'The Lady of the House of Love' is as predatory as the Marquis in 'The Bloody Chamber'.

'Puss-in-Boots' is very different from the other tales in the collection. It is Rabelaisian romp which would not be out of place in Chaucer's *The Canterbury Tales* or Boccaccio's *Decameron.* There are clear links to 'The Miller's Tale', in that the young wife's old husband cannot satisfy her sexually:

> Poor, lonely lady, married so young to an old dodderer with his bald pate and his goggle eyes and his limp, his avarice, his gore belly, his rheumaticks, and his flag hangs all the time at half mast indeed; and jealous as he is impotent …

Chaucer's old husband is described thus:

> Jalous he was, and heeld hire, narwe in cage,
> For she was wylde and yong, and he was old,
> And demed himself been lik a cokewold.

Just like Alison of 'The Miller's Tale', the wife is "in cage" because she is "behind so many bolts and bars you wouldn't believe". Marina Warner has noted that Carter is capable of "virtuoso reworkings of Chaucerian and Shakespearian comedy", in her essay 'Angela Carter: Bottle Blonde and Double Drag'.[2] The links between Chaucer and Carter are evident, and 'Puss-in-Boots' shares the idea that sex is fun for both genders, and that females are far from passive. As Danielle M. Roemer and Cristina Bacchilega write in their introduction to *Angela Carter and the Fairy Tale:* "Carter also interrogates Disney's habit of disempowering his female characters by allowing her own young woman character … to participate fully in the bed-thumping sex."[3] Not only does the young wife participate, she also takes the initiative in their second encounter. She "heaves him up and throws him on his back, her turn at the grind now and you'd think she'd never stop". This takes place upon the floor as the bed holds her dead husband, who has fallen down the stairs, after tripping over the female cat of the household, with whom Puss has begun a love affair. The fact that the two cats have planned this together shows that females too can be conniving and even cruel. These are not attractive traits, but within the context of the story, the reader finds it acceptable because the old man is a cruel miser. Carter is not claiming females are blameless.

Puss and his master gain access by pretending to be a rat-catcher and his cat, which allows Carter to create some entertaining and bawdy *double entendres* to add to the fun. When the "hag" returns to the bedchamber after the rat-catching is over, she asks why the sheets are so messy. Puss and his feline female have been catching rats while the master has been scoring "an instant bullseye". The reply from the wife is loaded with double meanings: "Puss had a mighty battle with the biggest beast you ever saw upon this very bed; can't you see the bloodstains on the sheets?" 'Puss' colloquially stands for the female (pussy)[4] and 'the biggest beast' for 'Signor Furioso', the pseudonym of the lover – a reference to his enthusiasm perhaps? The bloodstains on the sheets indicate loss of virginity. Of all the stories, this one is the most straightforward: apart from the fact that its narrator is a cat, it is the least like a fairy story. The cat and his master share a similar relationship to that of Casanova and his servant.[5] The attitude towards sex is that it is a healthy pleasure and can be enjoyed without scruple providing both the participants are willing. Other stories in the collection offer a more complex view.

One of the strangest tales 'The Snow Child' is also the briefest. To summarise the plot seems reductive. It has a doubly tripartite structure: the child is born of the Count's three wishes and dies of the Countess' third request. The count dismounts from his horse and rapes the corpse of the strange child, which melts and returns to the substances it was made from: snow, blood and a raven's feather. The Count gives his wife the rose the child died picking. It bites her. It sounds absurd as plot, but under Carter's magical surefootedness of style it attains the authority of a fable.

One of the most striking things about 'The Snow Child' is the winter setting which represents the Countess' coldness and her unwillingness or inability to have a child. It also signifies the virginal innocence of the child. It is the Count who longs for a child, whereas in most of the extant versions of the traditional story, it is the wife wishing for a child as "white as snow", "red as blood" and so on. The "hole filled with blood" which inspires his wish for "a girl as red as blood" could represent the menses, and the consequent disappointment that a pregnancy is not under way. By contrast the Count is "virile". Because the child has nothing to do with her, the Countess hates her and tries to dispose of her, rather like the stepmother in the fairy-tale versions of Snow White. Each request of the Countess' backfires and leaves her without first her furs and then her boots. It is the plucking of a winter rose which "kills" the snow child. A rose is often used as a sexual symbol, for example in an old ballad, 'The Bunch of Thyme',[6] where a deflowered maiden loses her "thyme" but is given a rose instead. Blake's poem 'The Sick Rose' from *Songs of Innocence and Experience* (1794), is often interpreted as being about sexual corruption.[7] The snow child is only an illusion and cannot cope with human maturation. Carter also refers to 'The Sleeping Beauty' here as the child pricks her finger (symbolising sexual penetration), "bleeds; screams; falls." Cristina Bacchilega also makes the connection with sexual maturity:

> By plucking the rose, the 'eternal' symbol of femininity in both its sexual and mystically sacrificial connotations, she comes of age – she bleeds – and then fulfils her function as passive object of the Count's desire.[8]

The Count's sexual invasion is unexpected and powerful as he "thrust his virile member into the dead girl" as though he is attempting to resuscitate her. It is not erotic sex, but businesslike: "he was soon finished." This copulation attempts to bring life, but has the opposite effect: "the girl began to melt". She was made of virginal snow. However, she leaves behind the rose, which "bites". Bacchilega sees this as demonstrating that: "In this snow-covered landscape, the only relationship possible between women is one that re-produces itself as rivalry, as struggles to survive at the other woman's expense."[9] Here Carter is drawing on the myth of *vagina dentata*, a vagina (the rose) has teeth which can bite. The *vagina dentata* myth arises from male fears that they will be swallowed up and destroyed by women. There are many myths from a several cultures which express the idea:

> 'Mouth' comes from the same root as 'mother' — Anglo-Saxon *muth*, also related to the Egyptian Goddess Mut. Vulvas have *labia*, 'lips,' and many men have believed that behind the lips lie teeth.[10]

The rose that bites is an ambiguous symbol: it may indicate that both the Snow Child and the Countess can protect themselves against men and against each other. The nub of the story is the battle between the Countess and the child. Perhaps the Countess only wins because she is real and has passed through puberty. The Count may be "virile" but his actions are ultimately reactive.

A feminist interpretation of this story would lead us to consider that the child may represent the Madonna type in the Madonna/whore dichotomy. The Countess is not a virgin and would demand to be pleasured and to be an active participant in sex, whereas the child is virginal and passive. The Countess' appearance, in furs, and boots with "scarlet heels, and spurs" indicates her status as a confident and assertive woman, the type men fear as well as desire, a dominatrix. The Count desires the virginal child as a sexual object, which suggests uncomfortable connotations of paedophilia and incest. Read in this way, the sex is perfunctory because the Count has no need to consider the virginal child as a participant with desires of her own. This is accentuated by the fact that she is "dead", which clearly implies necrophilia, a link to the bloody chamber of the Marquis in the title story. She melts away because she has satisfied his desire and her purpose is at an end. The snow child represents a concept about which men fantasise though it cannot exist in the real world. Carter is showing her readers that the Madonna/whore opposition is reductive.

Another story which uses the symbol of the rose in a sinister way, which again recalls Blake's 'The Sick Rose' poem, is 'The Lady of the House of Love'. Lorna Sage notes that the title connotes a brothel:

> The other implication of this story's title – The House of Love as brothel (indeed it reminds its chaste hero of a necrophiliac tableau in a brothel in Paris) – alludes short-hand style to the bargain involved in marriage and/or prostitution.[11]

This reference to 'The Bloody Chamber' title story prompts the reader to link the Marquis to the Lady Vampire in a neat gender reversal. An innocent young bicyclist is seduced by her and led to her bedchamber, as countless "shepherd boys and gypsy lads" have been before him. The vampire seems passive but is in fact a seductress who adopts a passive appearance to disarm her prey. Carter makes her domination clear: "Now she is a woman, she must have men". Ironically, her only dress is a wedding dress, but she is a travesty of a bride. Into her decadent house comes an antithesis to her: "a young officer in the British army, blond, blue-eyed, heavy-muscled". We are told he not only possesses "the special quality of virginity" but also ignorance combined with power, and he is "rational". He opposes a decayed and dying old order by representing the new one, symbolised by his bicycle, a nineteenth-century invention, and the fact that he is destined to fight in the First World War, an event which will sweep away the old order. The red roses which surround the vampire's mansion are overtly sexual, "inducing a sensuous vertigo ... faintly corrupt ... whorled, tightly budded cores outrageous in their implications". His bicycle is taken "to the entrails of the mansion". It is as if he is entering the body of a woman. The Countess herself is a contradiction: armed with "the pentacle of his virginity" he feels moved to pity by her "waiflike" eyes, yet her "wide, full, prominent lips of a vibrant purplish-crimson" echo the overbearing roses. He is partly repelled, partly attracted, but his innocence keeps him free from fear. He feels it would be wrong to have sex with her as she is so clearly frail and, he imagines, consumptive: "How can he now take criminal advantage of the disordered girl with fever-hot, bone-dry, taloned hands and eyes that deny all the erotic promises of her body ...?" His virginity and compassion save him. She becomes human, and therefore dies, when he kisses her wound better after she has pricked herself with broken glass. This pricking is an aspect from 'The Sleeping Beauty' which has been transformed by Carter into the agent of death rather than sleep. However, the dead vampire leaves a rose, a "dark fanged rose ... plucked ... from between my thighs", which the man takes away with him. At the end of the story the rose, which he has revived by placing its almost dead head in water, foreshadows the bloodletting of the trenches. He has been saved by his innocence once, but it cannot protect him against the engines of war.

The vampire uses the appearance of passivity to prey on her victims but there are clear links between her and the Marquis of 'The Bloody Chamber'. Both prey on the innocent, seducing them by offering them what they want – in the case of the vampire, sex; in the case of the Marquis, a prestigious marriage, money and a life of luxury. The vampire character shows that women are just as likely as men to prey on the opposite sex. It is not an attractive picture, but it is realistic. Carter is opening up discussion through the way the tales counterbalance one another and present contrasting outcomes and characters.

If the vampire reminds the young hero of a scene in a brothel, in which a "customer" could have sex with "a naked girl upon a coffin", then the Marquis has created a real version of this scene in his secret room:

> The opera singer lay, quite naked, under a thin sheet of very rare and precious linen, such as the princes of Italy used to shroud those whom they had poisoned.

One of the most disturbing things about this corpse is the fact that it is smiling, and therefore may have been a willing participant in an act of sadomasochism. However, the smile could also be one of agony. The close parallels between the scenes in these two stories – the one, an appearance only, a piece of play-acting, and the other deadly real – invites the reader to make the link between the tales and perceive the careful design of the collection.

The violence that has been committed against the wives of the Marquis also reflects the way society labels and silences females. The opera singer has been strangled because her gift was her voice; the Romanian countess, 'a lady of high fashion', has been pierced by a "hundred" spikes in the iron maiden, to destroy her body; the wife with the beautiful face, the artist's model, is now a stripped skull suspended in mid-air and "crowned" with a bridal veil. A woman's voice, a woman's body and a woman's face are all aspects which society values, but are not to do with a woman's intelligence or personality. The Marquis plans to behead the disobedient fourth wife because she is no further use to him. Her planned decapitation indicates she has been chosen for her intelligence as well as her innocence.

The Marquis has a taste for sadistic pornography. The young wife visits his library, which sounds like a bibliophile's dream, with its "row upon row of calf-bound volumes", apple-wood fire and cosy chairs. But there are strong clues to his depravity. Husymans' *Là-bas* is on a lectern, "bound like a missal". This novel's subject is occultism and the black arts, including the Black Mass. The protagonist of this novel is researching Gilles de Rais, a fifteenth-century

French marshal, who he discovers may be the source of the Bluebeard stories, a cunning use of intertextuality from Carter, since 'The Bloody Chamber' is a text transformation of 'Bluebeard'. The book includes sickening violence and is a classic horror text. In the bookcase the fourth wife of this decadent Marquis opens an untitled volume to find a picture of a young girl about to be whipped as a punishment for curiosity, exactly the fault the protagonist narrator is tempted to commit later in the story. Carter uses Anglo-Saxon lexis to shock the reader:

> … the girl with tears hanging on her cheeks like stuck pearls, her cunt a split fig below the great globes of her buttocks, on which the knotted tails of the cat were about to descend, while a man in a black mask fingered with his free hand his prick, that curved upwards like the scimitar he held.

Further engravings in the book, not described in detail, are even more horrific: "enough to make me gasp". When the Marquis discovers her looking at these texts, he makes a further reference to religion when he calls her a "little nun" and the books "prayerbooks". In his unholy religion, the pornographic texts are his bible, and the bloody chamber is his church. It is his discovery of her looking at these books which precipitates his taking of her virginity, which implies that his jaded appetite needs the stimulation of pornography to perform. In an earlier scene, he stripped her but did not attempt sex. He is presented as a man who sees women as objects. This notion is furthered by his inspection of his "purchase". The wife herself makes the link to the brothel: "… a formal disrobing of the bride, a ritual from the brothel". The cynical approach of the Marquis to sex is in direct opposition to the young people in 'Puss-in-Boots'.

In these stories, Carter presents sex in a range of ways. She juxtaposes the healthy with the depraved, leaving the reader in no doubt of the willingness of the female to enjoy sex. Female passivity is distasteful. Her writing about sex is analytic, not erotic.

Notes

1 *Essays on the Art of Angela Carter: Flesh and the Mirror*, edited by Lorna Sage, Virago, 1994.

2 Ibid.

3   *Journal of Fairy Tale Studies*, 12, 1 (1998), issue on 'Angela Carter and the Literary *Märchen*' (guest editors: Cristina Bacchilega and Danielle M. Roemer). Reprinted in *Angela Carter and the Fairy Tale*, Wayne State University Press, 1998.

4   According to *Womanwords* by Jane Mills (Virago, 1991), "In 1664 pusse emerged as coarse slang for vagina, and in this sense puss is akin to the Old Norse puss, meaning pocket or pouch."

5   *Histoire de ma vie* (1794), first fully published by F.A. Brockhaus, Wiesbaden and Plon, Paris, 1960

6   Once I had a bunch of thyme.
    I thought it never would decay,
    Then came a lusty sailor who chanced to pass my way,
    And stole my bunch of thyme away.

7   O Rose, thou art sick!
    The invisible worm
    That flies in the night,
    In the howling storm,

    Has found out thy bed
    Of crimson joy:
    And his dark secret love
    Does thy life destroy.

8   *Postmodern Fairy Tales: Gender and Narrative Strategies*, University of Pennysylvania Press, 1997.

9   Ibid.

10 From *The Woman's Encyclopaedia of Myths and Secrets* by Barbara Walker, Harper, 1983.

11 'Angela Carter: The Fairy Tale', *Journal of Fairy Tale Studies*, 12, 1 (1998). Reprinted in *Angela Carter and the Fairy Tale*.

4

But it was No Longer a Wolf's Paw

One of the most significant motifs in these stories is transformation. This is fitting, as transformations have long been a part of storytelling and mythology. Humans seem to be fascinated with the links we have with the animal kingdom. Elizabethan and Jacobean dramatists frequently use animal imagery to indicate evil, for example Goneril in *King Lear* is described as "wolfish"[1] and the hesitant Macbeth asked by his shrewish wife, "'what beast was't then/That made you break this enterprise to me?'"[2] The Latin poet Ovid retells many of the Greek transformation myths in his *Metamorphoses*, completed in AD 8. These transformations are frequently those of humans into animals, such as Arachne who became a spider. The werewolf myths are also very ancient and are among the most potent of transformational creatures. They developed gradually, being added to and embroidered over time, and taken up by many writers, including Carter. Ovid includes werewolves in the *Metamorphoses*.[3] The notion could be seen as a way of symbolising the animal instincts which inhabit every human, what Freud called the 'id'.[4] Anny Crunelle-Vanrigh writes that Carter's tale 'The Werewolf' "discloses the animal at the heart of the human".[5] Fairy stories often feature anthropomorphic creatures who can speak and behave like gentlemen, but who have the appetites of animals. The wolf in 'Little Red Riding Hood' is one example. This particular story and its variants can be seen as a warning to young girls not to trust strange men, however amiable they may appear, and not to stray from the path, or disobey their parents. Perrault, for example, concludes his version of 'Little Red Riding Hood' with:

> a lengthy moral ... in which he warns little girls to beware of not only "real wolves with hairy pelts" but also of "wolves who seem perfectly charming ... [yet who] are the most dangerous beasts of all".[6]

Carter chooses not to present girls in such a passive way, and the reader finds the heroines countering dangers in brave and resourceful ways, in some cases joining forces with the wolves. The group of stories placed at the end of the collection focuses on werewolf transformations, but there are also elements of transformations in other stories, mostly notably 'The Tiger's Bride' and 'The Courtship of Mr Lyon'. There are three feline stories and three lycanthrope stories – part of the balance Carter builds into the collection. The third feline story is 'Puss-in-Boots', which is not a transformation story, but rather a tale narrated by an anthropomorphic character. 'The Werewolf' and 'The Company of Wolves' are directly concerned with werewolves, whereas 'Wolf-Alice' is not a wolf at all, but a feral child who becomes less wolf-like as the tale progresses. 'The Werewolf' and 'The Company of Wolves' are placed together in the collection; both allude to 'Little Red Riding Hood'. 'The Snow Child' is a different type of transformation: snow into a child and back again, rather than involving beasts. The balanced structure of the collection is part of Carter's discussion and exploration of human nature, by presenting the reader with alternatives.

So what are werewolves? They are mythological humans who transform into wolves at full moon. They prey on humans and can only be killed by a silver bullet. Being bitten by a werewolf can pass on the condition. The eyes are red, and a person must be unclothed in order to transform. Carter works within these parameters, and exploits them in a range of interesting ways. In 'The Werewolf', the grandmother herself is the shape-shifter. When the wolf first appears in the story, the reader is expecting it and the description fits in with the above conventions: "It was a huge one, with red eyes, and running, grizzled chops." However, the reader's expectations are confounded. The young girl, the Little Red Riding Hood figure, defends herself, and in doing so, strikes off a paw. Grandmother's house is not the refuge we might hope: it is the very home of the werewolf. The paw is transformed into a hand which the child recognises as her grandmother's. Further evidence is provided by her grandmother's illness, a fever from the infected stump. This story can be read as a fable about the next generation taking over from the previous one, especially as the child takes over her grandmother's house after she is killed by the local people for being a witch. As Cristina Bacchilega puts it in her study, *Postmodern Fairy Tales* (University of Pennsylvania Press, 1997):

> She replaces the old woman, not by assimilation but through a violent severance that reproduces the wolf's ferocity. As the narrative comes to a close, the ambiguous implications of the girl's possession of her grandmother's house allow for no easy moral judgement or unmediated explanation. Has she defeated the witch? Turned into one herself? Both or neither?

The mother has sent her out, armed with a knife as if to seek her fortune, to make her own way in the world and pass the tests she may face. The wolf does try to attack her; therefore she is justified in her reaction. But the terrifying werewolf is, after all, just a frightened old woman whom the child exposes as a shape-shifting witch. Carter casts doubt on whether the old woman is really dangerous by setting the story in the context of superstitious people who believe in the devil and fear witches:

> When they discover a witch – some old woman whose cheeses ripen when her neighbours' do not, another old woman whose black cat, oh, sinister! *follows her about all the time,* they strip the crone, search her for marks, for the supernumerary nipple her familiar sucks. They soon find it. Then they stone her to death.

The local people convict the grandmother on the strength of the wart on the severed hand, not on a sighting of her as a werewolf. Carter's ironic tone: "They knew the wart on the hand at once for a witch's nipple". shows her cynicism about the evidence used against old women condemned as witches in the past. The neighbours are responsible for the execution, not the 'child', but it is interesting that the 'child' does not return home to her mother. She profits from the old woman's death. Carter leaves the reader disturbingly in doubt about who is dangerous and who is endangered.

The 'child' is also transformed. At first, she is cast in the role of a sacrificial victim, wearing "a scabby coat of sheepskin" and sent by her mother into certain danger, alone in a harsh forest where, according to local beliefs, witches, wolves and vampires abound. The hunted becomes hunter when the child is able to attack the wolf and save herself as she "seized her knife and turned on the beast". At the end of the story, she is living an independent existence, though still referred to as a 'child'. The old woman, the hunter in wolf form, becomes the hunted and the scapegoat. This reverses their roles, just as children grow to reverse roles with the older generation. Interestingly, too, there are no male characters mentioned, save the Devil and a father present only by virtue of the fact she has "her father's hunting knife". The three female characters, the child, the mother and the grandmother, are all different generations of the same family. They are all presented as tough and detached from any tender feelings for one another. Carter has radically departed from the nursery tale of 'Little Red Riding Hood', much as Carol Ann Duffy does in her poem 'Little Red Cap' where the child slays the beast she has loved, once she has outgrown him.[7] Both Carter and Duffy use the nursery tale as a basis for a rite of passage story, a *Bildungsroman* in miniature.

'The Company of Wolves' has many links with 'The Werewolf'. It can also be seen as an initiation story, but this time the child explicitly reaches womanhood and loses her virginity to the wolf. The wolf and the huntsman of the nursery tale are united in one being, and, as in some versions of the tale, she meets him for the first time when he appears to be charming and solicitous. Before the reader encounters the Little Red Riding Hood character, a range of information is given about werewolves, in which Carter draws on the conventions outlined above. The language is heightened and figurative: for example, the eyes of the wolf

> shine like candle flames, yellowish, reddish, but that is because the pupils of the eyes fatten on darkness and catch the light from your lantern to flash it back to you – red for danger; if a wolf's eyes reflect only moonlight, then they gleam a cold and unnatural green, a mineral, a piercing colour.

The use of colour is deft here: it is hard to say which is the more chilling, the red eyes of a wolf who sees its prey, or the cold, hard eyes of a hungry wolf. "Fatten" implies eating, and "piercing" suggests wounding, indicating the creature's intention. The writing is very visual; in the same passage, the metaphor, "luminous terrible sequins stitched suddenly on the black thickets", is striking. Like eyes, sequins are reflective and will suddenly come into view as the light catches them. The use of sibilance, combined with the consonance of the 'ck' sound, help to summon up the horror that a "benighted traveller" would feel if he or she saw a wolf's eyes in the dark of the wood, as the strong consonants of the 'ck' sound suggest the thickness of the forest, and the unlikelihood of escape. Carter describes the wolves as "'shadows … wraiths … grey members of a congregation of nightmare", using anaphora by repeating "they will be", thus giving this rule of three (hendiatris) a hypnotic and cumulative effect. She describes their howl using words drawn from music such as "song" and "aria", which accentuate the horror by contrast.

From this detailed description, Carter moves into brief anecdotes, such as stories of a "grey famished snout questing under the door" and a woman "bitten in her own kitchen as she strained the macaroni". The mundane detail of "macaroni" creates a sense of realism. The anecdotes become more developed and detailed, all building suspense, to illustrate what wolves can do, and to deepen our belief in them. This part of the story is rounded off with further advice on how to avoid being caught. The situation is nicely set up for the story, with the reader primed for horror, their expectations heightened.

Carter employs further conventions of the horror story. The heroine is portrayed as delicate and vulnerable, a stereotypical maiden in need of rescue, ill equipped to survive without protection: "… so pretty and the youngest of her family, a little late-comer". She is just on the cusp between child and woman, with very fair hair and "scarlet and white" cheeks. The red and white colour contrasts associated with her mark her out as an innocent, sacrificial, virginal maiden, much like Tess in Hardy's great novel, whose white dress and scarlet ribbon, among many other uses of these two colours, subliminally signal her fate to the reader.[8] Carter describes the girl's new red shawl as having "the ominous if brilliant look of blood on snow". The reader is told explicitly that she has just started menstruating, and a range of metaphors is used to foreground her virginity, such as "a sealed vessel", "pentacle" and "unbroken egg". The latter suggests vulnerability but the "pentacle" is protective. She is made to seem all the more vulnerable by the fact that she is ignorant of danger. The simile which has the forest swallowing her "like a pair of jaws" suggests she is likely to be devoured there. She disobeys her father's rule to travel through the forest to her grandmother. She is asserting herself as a woman, and passing from childhood to womanhood by means of her disobedience. She is attracted by the young man she meets, who is described positively by Carter: "… a very handsome young one, in a green coat and wideawake hat of a hunter … a flash of white teeth … she'd never seen such a fine fellow before." Carter has told the reader to beware naked men as they may be werewolves, and we are reassured, along with the heroine, that he is perfectly safe. Furthermore, we expect him to protect her, as he has a rifle and a compass. Carter adds a rather disturbing detail at this point: "He laughed at her again; gleaming trails of spittle clung to his teeth." Subtly, Carter suggests that this personable young man is in fact the werewolf to be feared, despite the trappings of civilisation he bears, and we are not disappointed. The two separate to see who will arrive first. Like the girl, the reader hopes the young man will: the reward for winning the bet is a kiss. Carter is playing tricks with the reader, as horror seems to turn to romance for a moment: "a rustic seduction; she lowered her eyes and blushed." Of course, reader expectation is not disappointed and he does reach grandma first. She is also treated to a seduction as the young man strips, and is described in an attractive manner. The narrative perspective is that of the old woman: "He strips off his trousers and she can see how hairy his legs are. His genitals huge. Ah! huge." She clearly appreciates his virility! Carter glosses over the consumption of grandmother and there is no suffering, only the sight of him approaching the bed, not yet a wolf: "The last thing the old lady saw in all this world was a young man, eyes like cinders, naked as a stone, approaching her bed." This sounds pleasurable, and the language of seduction continues to be used as he sets the scene for the girl, changing the sheets, plumping the pillows and tidying away the bones. He is still referred to as a man, though the reader knows what he is and is in complicity with him as he waits for her, dressed in grandmother's night clothes. Once she arrives, he calls her "darling" repeatedly. The traditional questions from the original fairy tale become a seductive game: 'What big arms you have./All the better to hug you with." The seduction continues, with Little Red Riding Hood fully willing and unafraid, eager to lose her virginity to the sexy young man. The link between her red shawl and her fate is made explicit: "… she shivered, in spite of the scarlet shawl she pulled around herself as if it could protect her although it was as red as the blood she must spill." This blood is not the blood of the wolf/man but of her maidenhead, willingly surrendered. At the start of the story she is said to draw the shawl over her head, which is symbolic of rebellion against her father, because in the French Revolution, the revolutionaries (and their supporters) wore red caps. Her father "might forbid her" and her mother cannot govern her; she is ready to shift for herself and find a husband. The man she meets in the forest is a cut above the local boys, a "fine fellow". As he moves in on his prey, his back against the door and her grandmother's hair burning in the fire, she realises she is "in danger of death" but in the mould of Carter heroines, she "ceased to be afraid" and instead is filled with sympathy for the wolves who howl outside in the cold. She is willing to follow his instructions and remove all her clothes. It is a bizarre marriage service with music provided by the wolves outside "howling in concert". As she gives him his kiss, she comments on his teeth, as the expected question and answer forms the dialogue: "What big teeth you have!". His jaw "begins to slather" but she holds her nerve, and finds the answer: "All the better to eat you with" amusing. It is as though both are engaged in a sexual game. It is she who then takes the lead and undresses him. Like the girls in the feline stories she is "nobody's meat". He is the one who is "fearful", and, in the morning, "tender". As can be seen in the title story of the collection, "tender" also refers to meat. By applying the word here to the wolf/man, the roles are reversed. The young girl has mastered the wolf/man and not the other way round. The white girl and the man with red eyes are married, "in a savage marriage ceremony". In some ways, this is more of a love story than a transformation story, as the young man never appears as a werewolf, though the reader is left in no doubt of his true nature. But she is his match. Whether she has made him more human or he has made her wolf-like is left for the reader to decide. It is not accidental that this story is immediately followed by 'Wolf-Alice', the story of a feral child raised by wolves. Carter blurs the line between man and monster, and shows that these qualities are within humans, that we are all part human and part beast. The transformative power of love is shown in many of these stories.

Notes

1 Act I, scene iv.

2 *Macbeth*, Act I, scene vii.

3 Book I, 199–243, where Lycaon is turned into a wolf.

4 'Das Es', or 'the it', is the brain function which includes the basic instincts, ungoverned by higher impulses, explored by Freud in *New Introductory Lectures on Psychoanalysis* (1933). 'Id' is a Latinised translation of the term into English. The other functions are the 'ego' and the 'superego'.

5 'The Logic of the Same and Différance: "The Courtship of Mr Lyon"', in *Angela Carter and the Fairy Tale*, Wayne State University Press, 1998.

6 *Fairy Tales of Charles Perrault 28*, cited by Elise Bruhl and Michael Gamer, in their essay 'Teaching Improprieties', from *Angela Carter and the Fairy Tale*.

7 *The World's Wife*, Picador, 1999.

8 *Tess of the d'Urbervilles*, Osgood, McIlvaine, 1891 (chapter 2: "She wore a red ribbon in her hair, and was the only one of the white company who could boast of such a pronounced adornment").

5

The Portals of the Great Pines

The traditional settings for fairy tales are twofold: interiors and exteriors. Comfortable interiors offer refuge from the dangerous world outside, although often these sanctuaries are less safe than they seem. For example, Hansel and Gretel find that the cottage made of sweets harbours a cannibalistic witch, and a wolf lies in waiting in grandmother's bed in 'Little Red Riding Hood'. There are oppositions to be observed in the interior spaces: in gorgeous palaces and castles and in hovels, an indication of the class structures of the time. The exterior spaces are dominated by woodland, and most stories involve a journey, often a quest, into that woodland. In *Into the Woods,* the 1986 musical by Sondheim and Lapine, for example, the woods are used as a symbol for all the risks that must be taken to reach one's goals in life.

> *Into the Woods*
>
> Without delay,
> But careful not
> To lose the way.
> Into the woods,
> Who knows what may
> Be lurking on the journey?
>
> Into the woods
> To get the thing
> That makes it worth
> The journeying.
> Into the woods –

The woods are full of dangers, particularly for those who stray from the path. They could be inhabited by all manner of creatures, including werewolves, witches and talking animals. Carter does not stray from tradition when devising the settings of her fairy stories, as she needs the symbolism they offer.

Her characters, in the same way as traditional characters, go through a process of change as they confront their innermost desires and find their real identity. In *The Bloody Chamber and Other Stories,* all of the settings are liminal[1] spaces to facilitate the rites of passage. As Terri Windling puts it in 'White as Snow: Fairy Tales and Fantasy,' in *Snow White, Blood Red,*[2]

> The fairy tale journey may look like an outward trek across plains and mountains, through castles and forests, but the actual movement is inward, into the lands of the soul. The dark path of the fairy tale forest lies in the shadows of our imagination, the depths of our unconscious. To travel to the wood, to face its dangers, is to emerge transformed by this experience.

So Carter shows her respect for the tradition by using its frameworks and conventions but subverting them by adding her own twists and angles. This acknowledgement of the fairy-tale genre allows her to draw fully on the storytellers who have gone before, and tap into our deepest instincts and fears. This strengthens her writing and allows her to pack a great deal of significance into the short stories of this collection, some of which are brief indeed, like 'The Snow Child'. In the novelette, 'The Bloody Chamber', however, she employs a modern setting, which she has the space to realise fully. 'The Lady of the House of Love' is set just prior to the First World War.

In the title story, 'The Bloody Chamber', the female narrator's journey, from the safety of home to the mortal danger of her new husband's gorgeous castle, from poverty to luxury and from innocence to experience, is by train. Carter has updated the setting, but a train is clearly liminal, moving, in this case through the night, from one place to another. The fact that it is a steam train with its "thrusting pistons" enables Carter to incorporate sexual undertone. The protagonist is passing from girlhood and virginity to maturity and marriage:

> ... I lay awake in the wagon-lit in a tender, delicious ecstasy of excitement my burning cheek pressed against the impeccable linen of the pillow and the pounding of my heart mimicking that of the great pistons ceaselessly thrusting the train that bore me through the night, away from Paris, away from girlhood, away from the white enclosed quietude of my mother's apartment, into the unguessable country of marriage.

Carter makes the journey sound ominous, as the metaphorical destination, marriage, is an unknown for the virginal bride. The physical destination is the stuff of fairy tales, a "sea-girt, pinnacled domain", which sounds like a castle in a picture book, although "girt", semantically related to girdle, suggests curtailment for the female, and "pinnacled" connotes a fortress. It is, moreover, "magic" and a "fairy castle whose walls were made of foam, that legendary habitation". It sounds insubstantial and beautiful, as well as unknown, heavy with the expectation of an heir and reeking of old money and all the snobbery that it entails. Carter emphasises the sea: it is important that the castle is cut off, isolated from any assistance for the young wife, who is to be pent up there like Rapunzel, away from society, in a beautiful prison. There is even a causeway; the place cannot be reached except when the tide is low. This detail helps to increase the tension at the end, since the narrator's mother must reach the causeway in time to save her daughter from being beheaded for disobedience.

The narrator's first view of the castle is even more beautiful than her expectations. Carter presents a list of its attributes, overwhelming the reader just as the young bride is overwhelmed:

> And, ah! his castle. The faery solitude of the place; with its turrets of misty blue, its courtyard, its spiked gate, his castle that lay on the very bosom of the sea with seabirds mewing about its attics, the casements opening on to the green and purple, evanescent departures of the ocean,

The loveliness of the description is essential to show why the bride allows herself to be seduced by the Marquis' wealth. The sounds and colours used are strongly evocative, and it is easy to overlook the "spiked" gate and the fact that fortresses can also be prisons. As the passage continues, the subtle hints of danger are made more potent. Its isolation is stressed: "cut off by the tide from land for half a day ...", as is its liminality, caught between the sea and the earth, yet belonging to neither:

> that castle, at home neither on the land nor on the water, a mysterious, amphibious place, contravening the materiality of both earth and the waves, with the melancholy of a mermaiden who perches on her rock and waits, endlessly, for a lover who had drowned far away, long ago. That lovely, sad, sea-siren of a place!

The imagery of mermaids and sirens has connotations of death and danger, and does not bode well for the narrator. Nor do the words which indicate sorrow, and the sibilant alliteration and consonance of the last line. Carter's narrator is young and innocent, only seventeen and not far removed from reading fairy stories at her mother's knee, so that the reader has to take into account her romantic perspective. For instance, she imagines herself "Queen of the Sea" in her turret suite. The castle, as well as being between sea and earth, is also caught between past and present. It is imbued with a sense of history and filled with mementoes of the Marquis' ancestors, exemplified by the portraits on the walls. The oxymoron of "anchored, castellated ocean liner" economically expresses its luxury and has powerful connotations of the *Titanic*, the doomed 1912 ocean liner which sank on its maiden voyage despite its state-of-the-art technology. However, it also boasts modern conveniences. This Breton castle is equipped with a telephone (although it is dead when the Marquise needs to use it to summon help), a grand piano, and the finest furnishings and rugs that money can buy. It is certainly "lush", as Carter hoped: "I wanted a lush fin-de-siècle décor for the story."[3] But all this luxury is a veneer which the narrator sees through little by little, first in the sadistic pornography and then in the bloody chamber itself, medieval in style, like a torture chamber.

The castle's wicked heart is central to the story, the bloody chamber itself, down a series of "ill-lit" corridors; like intestines, they "wound downwards … the viscera of the castle", decorated with tapestries of horrific scenes which hint at the contents of the forbidden room. Picked out in candle-flame, the pictures seem more disturbing:

> The flame picked out, here, the head of a man, there, the rich breast of a woman spilling through a rent in her dress – the Rape of the Sabines, perhaps? The naked swords and immolated horses suggested some grisly mythological subject.

These tapestries link back to the other paintings in the castle, such as "Moreau's great portrait of his first wife, the famous *Sacrificial Victim* with the imprint of the lacelike chains on her pellucid skin". The reader is reminded of these on the approach to the room where the body of his first wife lies on a "catafalque, a doomed, ominous bier", with the marks of her strangling on the cold white skin.

The bloody chamber is contrasted sharply with the rest of the castle. The door is "worm-eaten" and thus signifies death. It is hidden in the rock the castle is built on, below sea level and therefore dungeon-like, and filled with the instruments of torture. No expense has been spared, just like in the rest of the castle, but here the cost is in the antiquity and rarity of the objects, and in precious human life. Fittingly, the room has to be lit by candles, and this detail allows Carter to reveal its horrors in snatches, and to employ colour contrasts between the white objects picked up in the flame from the taper and the black darkness of the room and the dark red of the blood. The opera singer's "white breast" and the skull of the second wife "crowned with a wreath of white roses, and a veil of lace" contrasts with the "Chinese red" of the jar that holds lilies identical to the ones in the narrator's bedroom, and the pool of blood from the iron maiden he had used to kill his third wife. Carter composes the scene visually, and it is easy to imagine it as a painting, linking back to those in the approaching corridor.

After her dreadful discovery, the narrator's perspective changes. There is not a single room in which she feels safe or at ease. In the time that she has descended to the subterranean chamber, darkness has fallen, indicating her hopeless situation:

> A thick darkness, unlit by any star, still glazed the windows. Every lamp in my room burned, to keep the dark outside, yet it seemed still to encroach on me, to be present beside me but as if masked by my lights, the night like a permeable substance that could seep into my skin.

She is caught in a trap and there is not even a "star" to symbolise hope of escape. The darkness will claim her as it claimed the other brides. The extensive sibilance here lends the description further resonance. After she is eventually rescued, she turns the castle into a school for the blind, burying or burning the contents of the room and sealing the door. This is a clever resolution, as, of the five senses, the one the Marquis tempted was sight. The blind piano tuner was the only servant who could see her plight, or did not turn his back on it. Blindness is presented as safe and innocent, acting as a protection from ugly spectacles.

The Marquis' castle is not the only glamorous but decadent interior in the collection, although it is the grandest. The mansions of 'The Lady of the House of Love' and 'Wolf-Alice' are like decayed versions of the Marquis' castle. All three owe something to Dracula's castle in Bram Stoker's 1897 novel *Dracula*. Dracula's castle is equally a fortress where the owner can imprison people: "on three sides it was quite impregnable"[4] like the Marquis', though not surrounded by sea. The house of each of Carter's vampires is in a similar state of decay. In *Dracula*, Jonathan Harker observes in his journal that a "wealth of dust … lay over all and disguised in some measure the ravages of time and moth".[5] The 'House of Love' is similarly dusty:

> The unlit chandelier is so heavy with dust the individual prisms no longer show any shapes; industrious spiders have woven canopies in the corners of this ornate and rotting place, have trapped the porcelain vases on the mantelpiece in soft grey nets.

The furnishings are also similarly moth-eaten: "She sits in a chair covered in moth-ravaged burgundy velvet at the low, round table." The young bicyclist is the Jonathan Harker figure who steps into this Gothic scene, his innocence, like Harker's, contrasting with the surrounding decay and corruption. In 'Wolf-Alice', the setting is less significant than the character development of the feral child. It is lightly sketched, with the details left for the reader's imagination, such as referring to it as "cobweb castle". 'The Lady of the House of Love' is given a more detailed setting, with "family portraits" and endless corridors. The approach to the house is obscured by roses; fittingly as the story has strong links with 'The Sleeping Beauty', but these roses are rank and threatening:

> A great, intoxicated surge of the heavy scent of red roses blew into his face as soon as they left the village, inducing a sensuous vertigo; a blast of rich, faintly corrupt sweetness strong enough almost, to fell him. Too many roses. Too many roses bloomed on enormous thickets that lined the path, thickets bristling with thorns, and the flowers themselves were almost too luxuriant, their huge congregations of plush petals somehow obscene in their excess, their whorled, tightly budded cores outrageous in their implications. The mansion emerged grudgingly out of this jungle.

Red roses are, of course, associated with love, but there is a strong suggestion of decay and decadence in the lexical choices of "corrupt" and "luxuriant". The active verbs, such as "intoxicated" (containing the root 'toxic'), "blew", "inducing", "bristling", make the roses, and in particular their scent, seem dangerous and threatening. The scent is a foretaste of the gas used to kill the enemy in the First World War: it "blew into his face", inducing "vertigo" in "a blast of rich, faintly corrupt sweetness strong enough almost to fell him". The roses, "obscene" with "whorled tightly budded cores", resemble female genitalia, and indeed, the "dark fanged rose" the young man takes with him to war was "plucked from between" the thighs of the lady vampire who tried to seduce him. Its fangs also link it to the pointed teeth of a vampire. The bicyclist is walking into danger but he sees only a refuge, a shelter for the night.

After the death of the vampire, in the clean light of morning the mansion is seen in a different way. The voice of her caged pet lark, which only sings occasionally, "but more often remains a sullen mound of drab feathers" is replaced by the "larksong" of free birds outside. Once the caged bird has got free, it perches on her coffin to sing "its ecstatic morning song". The ironic play on the word "mourning" shows that, far from mourning the dead vampire, the lark is overjoyed by its new freedom. Light and air are let in through the windows by the bicyclist, and this reveals "how tawdry it all was". Everything was fake: "the catafalque not ebony at all but black-painted paper stretched on struts of wood, as in the theatre". The roses have lost their petals and as the wind blows them around the room, Carter uses the word "residue" which, allied to the colour "crimson" suggests blood. The early morning light seems harsh as it enters the chamber, with further connotations of war in the metaphor "fusillades". He has survived one possible death only to head off to one far worse, whose horrors can only be hinted at in the closing line: "Next day his regiment embarked for France."

Not all the mansions and castles of the rich hide dangers; Carter tends to set up oppositions in the settings just as she does in the plots. Mr Lyon's house is as beautiful as it seems. When Beauty's father first arrives there, it is winter, and the whiteness of the scene hints at not only the innocence but the lack of love within:

> Behind wrought iron gates, a short, snowy drive performed a reticent flourish before a miniature, perfect, Palladian house that seemed to hide itself shyly behind snow-laden skirts of an antique cypress.

Palladian houses are usually white, and the combination of the architectural style with the snowy scene creates an overall impression of dazzling whiteness, offset by the dying light. There is an air of sadness in the "reticence" of the building and the "antique cypress" with its associations of mourning and the underworld in Greek mythology. There are notes of danger, in the too-loud clanging of the gate, the lion's-head knocker, the door that opens on its own. Food is waiting for him, with *Alice in Wonderland* instructions such as '*Drink me*', and the beef on the sandwiches is "still bloody". The house and its contents are personified: for example the chandeliers emanate a "pleased chuckle". The single rose, discovered in the garden by the accidental brushing away of snow as Beauty's father leaves, is white. It is the theft of this rose, for Beauty, which sets the plot in motion. White roses are associated with innocence and purity. Beauty has requested a white rose as a gift from her father because material things mean nothing to her. She too is pure and "made of snow". Mr Lyon is fabulously wealthy, like the Marquis in 'The Bloody Chamber', but his outward appearance of an animal belies his good nature, whereas the Marquis' outward respectability belies his true inner evil.

Beauty eventually rescues Mr Lyon through love, but not before she has undergone her own rite of passage by being tempted by, but at last resisting, the materialism of the outside world. The drift of petals in the closing line of 'The Courtship of Mr Lyon' indicates nothing more sinister than the passage of time, the happy years spent together shown through the age of the pet spaniel. This setting is exceptional in that it does eventually provide a refuge for Beauty. However, in the contrasting tale, 'The Tiger's Bride', the "palazzo" of the tiger is "half derelict" and built in "red brick". All is disrepair, comfortless and uninhabited by humans. At the end of the story, the building collapses, and the two animals, the tiger and his bride, revert to nature.

Palaces and castles, then, offer little refuge from the horrors outside, in the woods of our subconscious. What then of hovels? The houses of the poor appear in only a few of these stories, and they are not described in detail. In 'The Company of Wolves', grandmother's house is poor, but cosy, with a rag rug on the tiles, a roaring fire, a bed set into the wall, and a pair of china spaniels on the mantelpiece. The door is unlocked, offering no protection from any creature that wishes to enter. In 'The Werewolf', the village people try to protect themselves by hanging "wreaths of garlic on the doors to keep out the vampires". The houses are sparsely furnished with only "A bed, a stool, a table". They are "built of logs, dark and smoky within". The same room is used for sleeping, cooking and storage. Religious icons suggest superstition on the part of the villagers rather than their civilisation. In 'The Werewolf' there is "a crude icon of the virgin behind a guttering candle", but in 'The Company of Wolves', its companion piece, the eyes of the werewolves are compared to candles, so that the small shrine seems to offer very little protection. The people who live in such dwellings have "cold hearts" to suit the coldness and harshness of their environment. Their attitude towards fairy-tale horrors is matter-of-fact: they expect to be exposed to them: "At midnight, especially on Walpurgisnacht, the Devil holds picnics in the graveyards and invites the witches; then they dig up fresh corpses and eat them. Anyone will tell you that." The harsh setting has produced these tough primitive people, who inhabit a world in which supernatural dangers are expected every bit as much as the natural dangers of the forest such as "bears" and "wild boar". The one-roomed houses are not always clustered together in a village; grandmother lives five miles away in the forest. They blend into the murky forests where paths and clearings are safer than the thickets of trees, but not by much.

The Erl-King, too, lives in a one-roomed house. It feels as if it is part of the wood enclosing it, "made of sticks and stones" with "grass and weeds" in the "mossy roof". Everything is made from the "bounty of the woodland", including the cages for the birds he has trapped. The house is neat and tidy, which disarms the reader because it seems safe:

> He is an excellent housewife. His rustic home is spic and span. He puts his well-scoured saucepan and skillet neatly on the hearthside, like a pair of polished shoes ...
> He hangs up herbs in bunches to dry, too – thyme, marjoram, sage, vervain, southernwood, yarrow. The room is musical and aromatic and there is always a wood fire crackling in the grate, a sweet, acrid smoke, a bright, glancing flame.

This description makes him sound like a fussy bachelor, but, as in the Marquis' castle, the attractiveness of the dwelling is a veneer. Its pleasant cosiness seduces, entraps. The girl knows he is dangerous, but seems happy to surrender to him, as though his power is part of the attraction: "He could thrust me into the seed-bed of next year's generation and I would have to wait until he whistled me up from my darkness before I could come back again." The temptation she feels is the desire to become part of the setting, to be subsumed into nature. She wants him to swallow her as if she were a "grain of corn"; she talks about "the stream I have become". Although she loves him, she has to kill him to save herself. He is weaving an "osier cage" for her, and she knows that the birds he keeps in cages are really "young girls" like herself. Being part of the landscape is an analogue for death, and she resists it. There is a strong link with the Greek myth of Persephone, who was taken to the underworld by Hades, to be his bride. Persephone was obliged to spend several months of the year in the underworld because she had eaten some pomegranate seeds during her stay there, thus explaining winter. The Erl-King is a Hades figure, but instead of being rescued, like Persephone, by her mother, the girl rescues herself by winning the Erl-King's trust.

The exterior spaces which feature most often in the stories in *The Bloody Chamber and Other Stories* are almost all woodlands and forests, discounting the gardens of the rich which are extensions of their mansions and castles. 'The Erl-King', 'The Werewolf' and 'The Company of Wolves' are all set in what feels to the reader like the same forest, the forest or woodland which is a traditional setting for folk tales and which must once have covered the countryside – as it still does in parts of Germany, where many of these tales originated. 'The Erl-King' is based in part on a European (possibly Danish) legend about a seductive but deadly archetype, similar to the fairy in Keats' 'La Belle Dame sans Merci', in which the knight is enchanted by a fairy who then vanishes, leaving him in despair.

In Carter's story, 'The Erl-King', the trees are close together, with "no way through the woods anymore", implying that there used to be a path at one time. This arouses the reader's curiosity. The wood seems like a living entity. It is secretive and imprisoning:

> Once you are inside it, you must stay there until it lets you out again for there is no clue to guide you through in perfect safety; grass grew over the track years ago and now the rabbits and foxes make their own runs in the subtle labyrinth and nobody comes.

The wood has a mind of its own; the "labyrinth" metaphor makes it seem deliberately obscure, a trap for a monster, as in the Greek myth of the flesh-eating Minotaur imprisoned in his labyrinth. The simile describing the wind,

> The trees stir with a noise like the taffeta skirts of women who have lost themselves in the woods and hunt round hopelessly for a way out,

prepares the reader for the young girls the Erl-King has trapped and turned into birds, and suggests ghostly inhabitants – girls who have perished when lost in the woods. Further into the story, when the girl is about to be trapped, the wind is mentioned again: "A wind rises; it makes a singular, wild, low rushing sound." In the famous poem 'Der Erlkönig' by the German poet Goethe (1749–1832), a boy carried by his father on horseback through the night hears the Erl-King tempting him to go with him. A wind springs up while the Erl-King is calling to the boy: "In dürren Blättern säuselt der Wind" (The wind rustles through dry leaves). Both the Goethe poem and the Carter story present the Erl-King as perilous: in Goethe:"Erlkönig hat mir ein Leids getan!" (the Erl-King has done me harm) and in Carter: "Erl-King will do you grievous harm." There is also a motif of music throughout both texts. The boy is tempted by the idea that the Erl-King's daughters will dance and sing and rock him to sleep. In the Carter text, in addition to the "diatonic spool of sound" that the Erl-King uses to snare birds, he possesses a stringless fiddle. The Erl-King will be strangled by the protagonist with his own hair, which the girl will then use to string the violin. She survives and sets free all the birds, which "change back into young girls", whereas in the Goethe poem, the Erl-King snatches the boy. When the father arrives at his destination, the child is dead.

For her ending, Carter draws on an old Scottish ballad collected by Francis Child, called 'Binnorie' in which one sister murders another out of jealousy. A harp is made from the dead sister's breast bone and strung with her hair. The harp plays a song which reveals the truth about the murder. Carter concludes her story in a similar manner:

> She will carve off his great mane with the knife he uses to skin the rabbits; she will string the old fiddle with five single strings of ash-brown hair.

> Then it will play discordant music without a hand touching it. The bow will dance over the new strings of its own accord, and they will cry out: "Mother, mother, you have murdered me".

This ending deliberately puts the reader in a state of confusion. Why does the music of the fiddle refer to the girl as "mother"? Or is it just a song? The Erl-King is portrayed as not meaning to harm; it is just his nature to do so: "in his innocence he never knew he might be the death of me." The protagonist is saving him from his nature by killing him, and she does so very tenderly, "with hands as gentle as rain". The setting seeps into every part of the plot. The Erl-King is a natural phenomenon: he is part of the forest and his seductive powers are part of nature.

In 'The Werewolf' and 'The Company of Wolves', the setting is in remote, cold northern forests full of wild beasts. Like the forest in 'The Erl-King', there is a sense of a living entity which can swallow people up. In "The Company of Wolves" the forest is "like a pair of jaws" which "closed" upon the young girl. The forest is also a source of entertainment to her:

> There is always something to look at in the forest – even in the middle of winter – the huddled mounds of birds ... the bright frills of the winter fungi on the blotched trunks of the trees ... the herringbone tracks of birds.

This presentation is enticing, similar to the enchanting sights in the forest of the Erl-King. Woodland also provides food. The Erl-King's larder is full of nature's bounty: "He makes salads of the dandelions ... and flavours them with a few leaves of wild strawberries ... sometimes he traps a rabbit." Similarly, in 'The Werewolf' and 'The Company of Wolves', the forests provide food and shelter: for example, the young hunter in the latter story, who turns out to be a werewolf, is carrying "carcasses of game birds". However, sometimes food is scarce, and then the werewolves look for humans to devour. The mood of the woods can change in an instant. Sometimes they are benevolent, and at other times menacing:

> Step between the portals of the great pines where the shaggy branches tangle about you, trapping the unwary traveller in nets as if the vegetation itself were in a plot with the wolves who live there, as though the wicked trees go fishing on behalf of their friends ...

The liminal landscapes of these stories allow the protagonists to move from a state of Innocence to a state of Experience, to complete the quests and undergo transformations which help them to find their inner resourcefulness and strength. Carter's settings both seduce and scare the reader.

Notes

1. Liminality is derived from the Latin *limen*, meaning 'threshold'. Liminal spaces are transitional, borderline and ambiguous.
2. William Morrow & Co., 1993, with Ellen Datlow.
3. Letter to a friend, quoted by Helen Simpson in *The Guardian*, 24 June 2006, in 'Femme Fatale', a review of *The Bloody Chamber*.
4. *Dracula*, chapter 3.
5. Ibid.

Further Reading

Cristina Bacchilega (ed.), *Postmodern Fairy Tales: Gender and Narrative Strategies* (University of Pennsylvania Press, 1997).

Cristina Bacchilega and Danielle M. Roemer (eds.), *Angela Carter and the Fairy Tale* (Wayne State University Press, 1998).

Ellen Datlow and Terri Windling (eds.), *Black Thorn, White Rose* (Avon Books (USA), 1994).

Lorna Sage (ed.), *Essays on the Art of Angela Carter: Flesh and the Mirror* (Virago, 1994).

J.R.R. Tolkien, *Tree and Leaf* (Allen & Unwin, 1964).

GREENWICH EXCHANGE BOOKS

STUDENT GUIDE LITERARY SERIES

The Greenwich Exchange Student Guide Literary Series is a collection of essays on major or contemporary serious writers in English and selected European languages. The series is for the student, the teacher and 'common readers' and is an ideal resource for libraries. The *Times Educational Supplement* praised these books, saying, "The style of [this series] has a pressure of meaning behind it. Readers should learn from that ... If art is about selection, perception and taste, then this is it."

(ISBN prefix 978-1-871551 applies unless marked*, when the prefix 978-1-906075 applies.)

The series includes:
Antonin Artaud by Lee Jamieson (98-3)
W.H. Auden by Stephen Wade (36-5)
Honoré de Balzac by Wendy Mercer (48-8)
William Blake by Peter Davies (27-3)
The Brontës by Peter Davies (24-2)
Robert Browning by John Lucas (59-4)
Lord Byron by Andrew Keanie (83-9)
Julius Caesar by Matt Simpson (37-8)
Samuel Taylor Coleridge by Andrew Keanie (64-8)
Joseph Conrad by Martin Seymour-Smith (18-1)
William Cowper by Michael Thorn (25-9)
Charles Dickens by Robert Giddings (26-9)
Emily Dickinson by Marnie Pomeroy (68-6)
John Donne by Sean Haldane (23-5)
Ford Madox Ford by Anthony Fowles (63-1)
Sigmund Freud by Stephen Wilson (30-9)
The Stagecraft of Brian Friel by David Grant (74-7)
Robert Frost by Warren Hope (70-9)
Patrick Hamilton by John Harding (99-0)
Thomas Hardy by Sean Haldane (33-4)
Seamus Heaney by Warren Hope (37-2)
Joseph Heller by Anthony Fowles (84-6)
Gerard Manley Hopkins by Sean Sheehan (77-3)

James Joyce by Michael Murphy (73-0)
Philip Larkin by Warren Hope (35-8)
Laughter in the Dark – The Plays of Joe Orton by Arthur Burke (56-3)
George Orwell by Warren Hope (42-6)
Sylvia Plath by Marnie Pomeroy (88-4)
Poets of the First World War by John Greening (79-2)
Philip Roth by Paul McDonald (72-3)
Shakespeare's *A Midsummer Night's Dream* by Matt Simpson (90-7)
Shakespeare's *Hamlet* by Peter Davies (12-5)*
Shakespeare's *King Lear* by Peter Davies (95-2)
Shakespeare's *Macbeth* by Matt Simpson (69-3)
Shakespeare's *The Merchant of Venice* by Alan Ablewhite (96-9)
Shakespeare's *Much Ado About Nothing* by Matt Simpson (01-9)*
Shakespeare's *Non-Dramatic Poetry* by Martin Seymour-Smith (22-6)
Shakespeare's *Othello* by Matt Simpson (71-6)
Shakespeare's *Romeo and Juliet* by Matt Simpson (17-0)
Shakespeare's Second Tetralogy: *Richard II–Henry V* by John Lucas (97-6)
Shakespeare's Sonnets by Martin Seymour-Smith (38-9)
Shakespeare's *The Tempest* by Matt Simpson (75-4)
Shakespeare's *Twelfth Night* by Matt Simpson (86-0)
Shakespeare's *The Winter's Tale* by John Lucas (80-3)
Tobias Smollett by Robert Giddings (21-1)
Alfred, Lord Tennyson by Michael Thorn (20-4)
Dylan Thomas by Peter Davies (78-5)
William Wordsworth by Andrew Keanie (57-0)
W.B. Yeats by John Greening (34-1)

FOCUS Series
James Baldwin: *Go Tell it on the Mountain* by Neil Root (44-6)*
William Blake: *Songs of Innocence and Experience* by Matt Simpson (26-2)*
Emily Brontë: *Wuthering Heights* by Matt Simpson (10-1)*
George Eliot: *Middlemarch* by John Axon (06-4)*
T.S. Eliot: *The Waste Land* by Matt Simpson (09-5)*
F. Scott Fitzgerald: *The Great Gatsby* by Peter Davies (29-3)*
Michael Frayn: *Spies* by Angela Topping (08-8)*
Thomas Hardy: *Poems of 1912–13* by John Greening (04-0)*
Thomas Hardy: *Tess of the D'Urbervilles* by Philip McCarthy (45-3)*
The Poetry of Tony Harrison by Sean Sheehan (15-6)*
The Poetry of Ted Hughes by John Greening (05-7)*
Aldous Huxley: *Brave New World* by Neil Root (41-5)*
James Joyce: *A Portrait of the Artist as a Young Man* by Matt Simpson (07-1)*

John Keats: *Isabella; or, the Pot of Basil, The Eve of St Agnes,
Lamia and La Belle Dame sans Merci* by Andrew Keanie (27-9)*
The Poetry of Mary Leapor by Stephen Van-Hagen (35-4)*
Harold Pinter by Lee Jamieson (16-3)*
Jean Rhys: *Wide Sargasso Sea* by Anthony Fowles (34-7)*
Edward Thomas by John Greening (28-6)*
Wordsworth and Coleridge: *Lyrical Ballads* **(1798)** by Andrew Keanie (20-0)*

Other subjects covered by Greenwich Exchange books
Biography
Education
Philosophy